WHAT TO DO WHEN
THE TEMPTER COMES

by
JOHN OSTEEN

Lakewood Church
P.O. Box 23297
Houston, TX 77228

ISBN 0-912631-16-3

WHAT TO DO WHEN
THE TEMPTER COMES

You have an enemy, the devil. He will try to tempt you and trick you in many areas of your life.

Do you know what to do when the tempter comes to you? The Bible gives some excellent examples of how to handle the tempter when he comes to deceive you, to confuse you, and to keep you from being the victorious Christian that the Lord intended you to be.

The tempter came to Jesus, and you are no exception. **If he came to Jesus he will surely come to you.**

You may ask, "Well, what shall I do when the tempter comes to me?"

You must find out what the Word of God says about the situation that the tempter has tried to put on you, and then do what the Word says to do to obtain victory.

Matthew 4:1-11 gives us a clear example of how the tempter tried to overcome Jesus, and how Jesus handled the situation. "Then was Jesus led up of the Spirit into the wilderness to be tempted of the devil. And when he had fasted forty days and forty nights, he was afterward an hungered. And when the tempter came to him, he said, If thou be the Son of God, command that these stones be made bread. But he answered and said, It is written, Man shall not live by bread alone, but by every word that proceedeth out of the mouth of God" (vss. 1-4).

Jesus was quoting the Word to the devil, "...man doth not live by bread only, but by every word that proceedeth out of the mouth of the Lord doth man live" (Deuteronomy 8:3).

"Then the devil taketh him up into the holy city, and setteth him on a pinnacle of the temple, and saith unto him, If thou be the Son of God, cast thyself down: for it is written, He shall give his angels charge concerning thee: and in their hands they shall bear thee up, lest at any time thou dash thy foot against a stone" (vss. 5-6).

The devil will quote Scripture to you. He was quoting Psalm 91:11-12, "For he shall give his angels charge over thee, to keep thee in all thy ways. They shall bear thee up in their hands, lest thou dash thy foot against a stone." And when he quotes Scripture to you, you are going to have to do what Jesus did. He quoted Scripture back to the devil.

"Jesus said unto him, It is written again, Thou shalt not tempt the Lord thy God" (Matthew 4:7). There are more Scriptures than one in the Bible that you can use against Satan. The devil will take the Scriptures and twist them to meet his purpose. But Jesus stayed right with the Word when He said, " It is written again..." He had another Scripture for the devil. "Ye shall not tempt the Lord your God..." (Deuteronomy 6:16).

You have to say to the devil, **"Devil, it is written again..."**

"Again, the devil taketh him up into an exceeding high mountain, and sheweth him all the kingdoms of the world, and the glory of them; And saith unto him, All these things will I give thee, if thou wilt fall down and worship me. Then saith Jesus unto him, Get thee hence, Satan: for it is written, Thou shalt worship the Lord thy God, and him only shalt thou serve" (vss. 8-10).

Another Gospel reads this way, "And Jesus answered and said unto him, Get thee behind me, Satan: for it is written, Thou shalt worship the Lord thy God, and him only shalt thou serve" (Luke 4:8). I prefer the translation in Matthew. It is bad enough having Satan standing in front of me, instead of having him behind me. I can just picture him standing right behind me, and getting ready to kick me. I don't like anybody behind me who is my enemy. In Matthew 4:10, Jesus said to Satan, "Get thee hence..." He was saying in other words, "Get out of my sight."

That same Scripture verse in The Amplified Bible says, "...Begone Satan! For it has been written, You shall worship the Lord your God and Him alone shall you serve" (Matthew 4:10).

"Then the devil leaveth him, and, behold, angels came and ministered unto him" (vs. 11).

BE CLOTHED WITH HUMILITY

Both Peter and James give us some excellent instructions concerning what to do when the tempter comes to you.

Peter tells us: "...be clothed with humility: for God resisteth the proud, and giveth grace to the humble. Humble yourselves therefore under the mighty hand of God, that he may exalt you in due time: Casting all your care upon him; for he careth for you. Be sober, be vigilant; because your adversary the devil, as a roaring lion, walketh about, seeking whom he may devour: Whom resist stedfast in the faith, knowing that the same afflictions are accomplished in your brethren that are in the world'' (1 Peter 5:5-9).

May I emphasize this: You do not have to find a strong preacher or a great personality to resist the devil for you.

YOU are to resist the devil and he will flee from you. That word **flee,** means "to run as if in terror."

YOU submit yourself to God.

YOU resist the devil, and he will flee from you.

James 4:6-7 says, "But he giveth more grace. Wherefore he saith, God resisteth the proud, but giveth grace unto the humble. Submit yourselves therefore to God. Resist the devil, and he will flee from you."

Both Peter and James talked about humility before they talked about resisting the tempter.

THE DEVIL IS NOT, AND NEVER HAS BEEN, IN HELL

I was once teaching on this subject and I made this statement: "The devil is not in hell, and he has never been in hell."

I was amazed. The people did not take issue with me, but they just said, "Is that so? Is that so?" That shocks a lot of new Christians when they hear that statement for the first time. They believe that Satan goes down into the fire and burns a while. Then he comes up to check out things on the earth. They have the idea that the devil goes down to hell and sits on a throne amid the flames.

No. The devil has never been in hell.

He is not in hell now, but he is going to hell. The Bible says that hell was created for the devil and his angels.

The devil is ruling as a ruler over the principalities and powers of the air. He is the god of this world. The Word tells us, "Put on the whole armour of God, that ye may be able to stand against the wiles of the devil. For we wrestle not against flesh and blood, but against principalities, against powers, against the rulers of the darkness of this world, against spiritual wickedness in high places" (Ephesians 6:11-12).

Paul also tells us, "But if our gospel be hid, it is hid to them that are lost: In whom the god of this world hath blinded the minds of them which believe not, lest the light of the glorious gospel of Christ, who is the image of God, should shine unto them" (II Corinthians 4:3-4).

SATAN CANNOT DEVOUR EVERY CHRISTIAN

The Holy Spirit says through Peter, "...the devil, as a roaring lion, walketh about, seeking whom he may devour" (I Peter 5:8). That Scripture verse indicates that Satan cannot devour everybody. He is legally bound in certain areas. He must obey the Word of God. He must bow to the Name of Jesus.

When Jesus came to earth, He went to the cross; He arose from the dead, and we are told in Ephesians 4:8-10, "Wherefore he saith, When he ascended up on high, he led captivity captive, and gave gifts unto men. (Now that he ascended, what is it but that he also descended first into the lower parts of the earth? He that descended is the same also that ascended up far above all heavens, that he might fill all things.)

Satan has to find a person who does not know anything about who he is as a new creature in Christ Jesus; about redemption; about the Name of Jesus Christ, and about the power of the Christian to use that Name.

It is important for us to know that we, as believers have the authority to use the Name of Jesus. Just before He was received up into heaven to sit at the right hand of God, Jesus told us in Mark 16:15-18, "...Go ye into all the world, and preach the gospel to every creature. He that believeth and is baptized shall be saved; but he that believeth not shall be damned. And these signs shall follow them that believe; In my name shall they cast out devils; they shall speak with new tongues; They shall take up serpents; and if they drink any deadly thing, it shall not hurt them; they shall lay hands on the sick, and they shall recover."

SATAN HAS NO RIGHT TO LORD HIS AUTHORITY ON EARTH OVER THE CHRISTIAN

Satan lorded it over me for years in the area of finances. I was dragging through life just barely getting along. I thought that it was very religious to be poor. In my ignorance the devil ruled and lorded poverty over me.

If you are ignorant of God's Word and God's will in any area, the devil will attempt to take advantage of you in that area.

If you do not know about healing for your body

or your mind, or your emotions, he will hold back God's blessing from you in those areas. He will tell you, "God did this to you...It is God's will for you to suffer..." But if you will get into the Word and find out what the Word says about the situation, Satan's lording it over you will come to an end.

Just as we are told in I Peter 5:9, "Whom resist stedfast in the faith..." we are told in James 4:7, "... Resist the devil, and he will flee from you."

THERE IS MORE THAN ONE WORLD

There are two worlds out there besides this one. There is the world where God reigns, and where the angels minister and hearken to His Word. That is the beautiful, wonderful, realm of spiritual reality where Jesus and the angels live.

There is also a spiritual realm where Satan lives with his demons, and where they have their activity.

Those places are places of reality. They are not just in our imaginations.

Some people say, "Well, you know there is supposed to be a spirit world out here somewhere. Maybe it exists and maybe it doesn't."

Know this: the spiritual world is a reality. Actually, the spirit world is more real than the physical world. Because God, Who is a Spirit, created the material world, He created it out of the spiritual realm. The Bible says, "Through faith we understand that the worlds were framed by the word of God, so that things which are seen were not made of things which do appear" (Hebrew 11:3). And John 1:1-3,10 says, "In the beginning was the Word, and the Word was with God, and the Word was God. The same was in the beginning with

God. All things were made by him; and without him was not any thing made...He was in the world, and the world was made by him, and world knew him not.''

Two spiritual forces vie for our attention. As we walk the pathway of life we are being influenced by one or the other. Influences come from another world. Satan and his demonic forces can hinder us. The Lord and his angelic forces can help us. Which force will you choose? It is up to you. The way you choose to be influenced will determine the quality of life that you live.

The devil makes it his business to use his demonic forces to tempt us, to discourage us, and to cause us to give up and be defeated.

Have you ever had a day when everything seemed to go wrong? I have had days when I just wanted to crawl back into bed and start over again. It seemed like there was an invisible pressure against me. I have said to my wife, Dodie, ''A spirit of confusion is here. Everything seems to be a flop. Everything seems to go wrong.'' When this happens, I have learned to call a halt to the service. I would immediately tell the devil to get out of that service, and he had to go.

The devil's business is to attack you. He wants to discourage you, and to tempt you. But you see, he cannot **make** you do anything.

There is a certain comedian who says, ''The devil made me do it!''

No! He cannot make you do anything unless he possesses you. He can work on your mind with a thought. He can try to get you to act against your will. He cannot transgress your own will, but he will try to deceive you.

DON'T GIVE IN TO THE TEMPTATION
OF THE DEVIL

Many sick people are tempted to give up when symptoms hang on. It looks like they cannot get healed. It looks like nobody can help them. It may look like the doctors have given up on them, and that their faith does not work. The tempter comes to them with those thoughts, and they will just give up their faith and say, "Well, I guess God has ordained that I should live this way."

That is a temptation. Don't give in to it.

OLDER PEOPLE ARE TEMPTED TO FEEL USELESS

Many elderly people are tempted to feel that their time of usefulness is over. Life becomes meaningless, and nobody cares. They will say, "My children don't care about me any more. I am no good in this life. I may as well give up and go on into eternity...After all, I am past seventy, and I am living on borrowed time anyway..."

That is not scriptural. The last time that God talked to His people about living a long life, He told them they were given one hundred and twenty years (Genesis 6:3). When God talked about four score years and ten, He was talking about the years of the Israelites in the wilderness (Psalm 90:10). But many people are tempted to say, "Well, you know that I am old; and I just can't do anything."

Colonel Sanders was a wonderful Christian businessman. He started his business (Kentucky Fried Chicken) at the age of sixty-five, and he was a success. He was in his nineties when he went to be with the Lord. In his latter years he started projects.

It is always good to be challenged by life. Have plans and some projects. When I am older, I want to be like

Caleb. He stood out there in the wilderness when he was eighty-five years old, and he looked at the toughest, highest mountain. He said to Joshua, "Give me this mountain." Caleb said in Joshua 14:10-14, "...behold, the Lord hath kept me alive , as he said, these forty and five years, even since the Lord spake this word unto Moses, while the children of Israel wandered in the wilderness: and now, lo, I am this day forescore and five years old. As yet I am as strong this day as I was in the day that Moses sent me: as my strength was then, even so is my strength now, for war, both to go out, and to come in. Now therefore give me this mountain, whereof the Lord spake in that day; for thou heardest in that day how the Anakims were there, and that the cities were great and fenced: if so be the Lord will be with me, then I shall be able to drive them out, as the Lord said. And Joshua blessed him, and gave unto Caleb the son of Jephunneh Hebron for an inheritance. Hebron therefore became the inheritance of Caleb..."

I am not looking for a rocking chair when I am old. I am looking for a mountain!

I believe that the potential, the ability, and the expertise of older people is in many instances being wasted. I believe that older people want to be useful. Why should we set people on the shelf when they get old enough to have some sense?

Many older people are tempted to say, "Well, you know, I am over the hill—around the bend. People don't want anybody who is seventy or seventy-five years of age."

Who said so? God can use you. Your spirit never grows old. Only your body grows old. You have eternal youth in your spirit man.

Ponce De Leon looked for the fountain of youth. I

would like to wake him up out of his grave and tell him, "I have found it! I have found eternal youth in the Lord Jesus Christ."

DIVORCED PEOPLE ARE TEMPTED TO FEEL DISQUALIFIED

I have found that people who are hard against divorce and broken homes sometimes end up divorced or have a broken home, or their children end up in trouble. We need to be careful and compassionate in what we say with our mouths about divorce. The people who have been divorced, and gone through all kinds of heartache in their lives, have had enough hurt without anyone's additional comments.

"Well," you say, "I know Jesus said..."

Yes, I know what Jesus said. It is a strange thing to me that we do not quickly take the Scripture as literally where Jesus said, "All liars shall have their part in the lake of fire."

We don't go around saying, "Well, you lied. You are going to hell." Christians will lie and then say, "Well, you know that God forgives..."

Well, doesn't God forgive divorce?

One man who was a preacher divorced his wife because of trouble—something that he could not help. He later said, "I should have shot her. The church will forgive murder more quickly that they will forgive divorce."

You may say, "But Brother Osteen, are you advocating homes breaking up?"

NO! I am against divorce. I do not think people should get a divorce, but when we find people who have been battered and bruised in life, they have had enough. Jesus commanded us to love them and help them. We are not to condemn them. Jesus said, "For God sent not his Son into the world to condemn the world: but that the world through him might be saved" (John 3:17).

Jesus once talked to a woman who had been married five times. He did not talk to her about giving up. He gave her life, and hope, and she went out to win the whole town.

Many divorced people are tempted by the devil to just give up. They feel disqualified, dirty, worthless, and undesirable.

Friends, we are not *for* all the things you have gone through. We are FOR LOVING YOU. We are FOR HELPING YOU. We are FOR ENCOURAGING YOU.

There once was a preacher who fell into sin. He broke up his home for another woman. Of course he was indeed wrong. There was no excuse for that, but the devil had deceived him.

The devil will tempt preachers, too. That preacher had prayed for people for twenty-five years; then he made one mistake and the devil got hold of him.

Instead of loving him, and helping him, the people criticized him. A very famous evangelist became so angry with him that he said, "I have over a million readers of my magazine, and I am going to expose him. I am going to put his name in there and tell the world what he has done." The evangelist was wrong. But he said, "I am going to write all about it, because this man is guilty."

The evangelist had his printing press all set up to expose the preacher to a million readers. Suddenly Jesus appeared to him and said, "You are going to expose him, are you?"

"Oh, yes!" the evangelist said. "I am, Jesus, because that man is guilty."

Jesus said, "Well, let me ask you a question: what if it were your son who was married, and this happened to him? Would you expose him?"

"Oh, no, Jesus!" he said, "I wouldn't do that, he is my son."

Jesus said, "Well, he is My son. You leave him alone!"

Oh, the immeasurable grace and love of God!

If you are a divorced person, do not give in to the temptation that you are useless just because your home has been broken.

MOST CONDEMNATION COMES FROM RELIGIOUS PEOPLE

People have come to me who have been living with another person for years. They have never married. They have just been living together for all those years. They come to church and they finally hear the truth. With all of their children, they say, "We are living in sin. We need to get married. Will you marry us?"

I say, "I sure will!"

Most condemnation comes from religious people. They want to make rules and laws that will bring people into the agony of some position that they cannot get out of.

Don't come to me with your ideas about dress codes. As long as people are decent, it is fine with me.

Don't tell me that wearing lipstick and makeup is wrong when God makes the red birds and blue birds!

People should quit trying to regulate the outside of men and women, and realize that God says in the Bible, "Man looketh on the outward appearance, but the Lord looketh on the heart" (I Samuel 16:7).

Which is worse? The outward appearance, or a

person who has an ugly, condemning spirit?

If Jesus were to give you the answer, I believe that He would say that the ugly spirit is worse.

The Bible says, "For I desired mercy, and not sacrifice" (Hosea 6:6).

I have found that if people are doing wrong you can love them into doing what is right. They will listen to you if you love them.

I am *for* the bruised.

I am *for* the broken.

I am *for* those who have been overtaken in homosexuality, lesbianism, alcoholism, and drug addiction.

Our business is not to condemn.

We are to tell them the Good News!

If you are one of those who has been tempted to give up because you have a broken home, don't give up.

If you have been overcome by some terrible habit, and the devil tempts you to give up, don't give up.

If you are in financial trouble, and you are tempted to live below God's plan for prosperity in your life, don't give up!

Young people are tempted to yield to things that will hurt and destroy them.

A young man who attended our church once was literally overcome by things in his life. He went home and shot himself. We did not have time to work with him and help him. He was overcome by that which hurts and harms.

Some young people say, "Well, you know, Brother Osteen is just an old 'fuddy-duddy.' He doesn't know what he is talking about. He and Dodie are over the hill..."

Well, we have been over a lot of hills, and we have learned a lot of things. I know this: when young people get out in a crowd they will be tempted to give in to peer pressure. They give in to this one, to that one, and to the other. The devil's business is to put pressure on you. He will tempt you to do what will hurt, harm, and destroy you.

Many young people are called of God. They see other people fail because of the vicissitudes of life. They are tempted to give up God's call on their lives. God's call is still there, but it grows dim to them. It is because the tempter has come to tempt them to give up the call of God.

Young person, the end of what the devil will tell you to do will bring nothing but sorrow. If you are tempted by the devil to give in, don't do it. Do not yield to temptation.

Jesus was tempted in all points of his life. We read in Hebrews 4:15, "For we have not an high priest which cannot be touched with the feeling of our infirmities; but was in all points tempted like as we are, yet without sin." And Hebrews 2:18 says, "For in that he himself hath suffered being tempted, he is able to succour them that are tempted."

The fact that Jesus was tempted in all areas of his life may encourage you when you are tempted. We will look at some of these areas where the tempter struck at Jesus, and what He did about it.

Number One: **Jesus' greatest temptation came after He was full of the Holy Ghost.**

The Word says, "Then was Jesus led up of the Spirit into the wilderness to be tempted of the devil" (Matthew 4:1). Jesus was thrust out into the world. It is God's plan that we know that we are walking on enemy territory. Satan is the god of this world. We must come face to face with the devil and the demon powers of this world. We can conquer!

Jesus was greatly tempted when He was full of the Holy Spirit.

I want to warn you. Don't get full of the Holy Ghost; don't get to be a fanatic; don't get to be a dancer and prancer, and a jumper and a shouter, and a quoter of the Word; and don't attend Charismatic or Full Gospel churches, if you do not want any trouble with the devil, because he is going to come after you. When he gives you a hard time say, "Well, hello there, Mr. devil. I have learned why you have come. I am so full of God that you can't stand it. So — just back up there. I am going to praise God for a while."

David said, "Thou (God) preparest a table before me in the presence of mine enemies..." (Psalm 23:5). The Lord will prepare you a table of victory right in the presence of the devil.

I like what Smith Wigglesworth said when he woke up one night, and felt a strange presence in his room. He looked over in the corner, and there stood Satan — in person. When Smith Wigglesworth saw him he said, "Oh, it's just you..." and he went back to sleep. That kind of an attitude will put the devil on tranquilizers. Many times we take the devil too seriously.

Number two: **Jesus was greatly tempted when He was about to enter into the plan of God for his life.**

When the Lord Jesus was just getting ready to step into his earthly ministry of signs, wonders, and miracles, and the marvelous plan that God had for him, the devil met him.

You are going to have the hardest battle just about the time you enter into the greatest time of victory that God has planned for you. If you are being greatly tempted today, it is because you are about to take that one step that will put you into the area that you have longed to be in.

Number three: **Jesus was tempted in the area of his need.**

This is so important. This will be a tremendous help to you. Jesus was tempted in the area of his need. He had fasted for forty days and forty nights. And He was hungry.

If you have ever fasted perhaps you can understand. I have never fasted that long. You do not have to fast for forty days and forty nights. I believe that the best way to fast is to fast a little bit every week. Maybe until three o'clock in the afternoon, or perhaps one day. It is important to continually keep your body under control and in subjection to your spirit man.

I haved fasted for several days, and I have noticed that I get to a place where hunger for food does not bother me. Then when the fast was over, there came a great hunger. When I knew it was time to eat, something just sprang into my being, and I could have eaten the plate, knife, fork, and everything on the plate.

Jesus was a natural human being. And when He finished that forty day fast every part of him was crying out for food. And the devil tempted him in the area of his need. "And when the tempter came to him, he said, If thou be the Son of God, command that these stones be made bread" (Matthew 4:3).

Has the devil tempted you in your area of need? Are you alone? Are you without a partner in life? Are you in financial need? The devil will tempt you in the area of your needs. He will say, "You see! God didn't tell you the truth, and all that preacher does up there is just tell lies. He is misusing the Scripture...You know that God doesn't want you to prosper."

The tempter will tempt you in the area where you are hurting the most.

I do not know your needs. It may be that you are sick in body. It may be that the doctors have said, "There is no hope."

Watch out! Right there is where the devil will hit you. He will come in and give you reasons in your mind that say it is God's will for you to die an early death. He will tell you that you are learning all kinds of "good lessons," while you are on the sick bed. He will tempt you to agree with that sickness, or in the area of your need.

Number four: **The devil tempted Jesus to disbelieve who He was.**

Jesus was and is the Son of God. And Satan knew it. Yet, he said, "If thou be the Son of God, cast thyself down..." (Matthew 4:6).

This is the way that the devil will put it to you: "Are you really a new creature? ARE YOU? You used a bad word the other day. You slipped and fell. Are you really born of God? Are you really an overcomer? Can you really do all things through Christ? Is this really true, 'Greater is He that is in you than he that is in the world'?"

He will tell you that you are a weak worm of the dust. When this happens just hit him with the Word.

Confess the Word of God:

I am a new creature in Christ Jesus.

The Word says, "For God so loved the world, that he gave his only begotten Son, that whosoever believeth in him should not perish, but have everlasting life" (John 3:16).

The Word says, "Therefore if any man be in Christ, he is a new creature: old things are passed away; behold, all things are become new" (II Corinthians 5:17).

The Word says, "For whatsoever is born of God overcometh the world: and this is the victory that overcometh the world, even our faith. Who is he that overcometh the world, but he that believeth that Jesus is the Son of God?" (I John 5:4-5).

The Word says, "I can do all things through Christ which stengtheneth me" (Philippians 4:13).

The Word says, "Ye are of God, little children, and have overcome them: because greater is he that is in you (me), than he that is in the world" (I John 4:4).

Number five: **The devil tempted Jesus to put somebody before God.**
Satan tempted Jesus to do foolish things in the name of religion — in the name of spirituality. He tempted Jesus to put someone before God, and to do foolish things in the name of serving God, He said, "...If thou be the Son of God, cast thyself down: for it is written, He shall give his angels charge concerning thee: and in their hands they shall bear thee up, lest at any time thou dash thy foot against a stone" (Matthew 4:6).
Jesus quoted Scripture to him, "...It is written again, Thou shall not tempt the Lord thy God" (vs.7).
The devil didn't stop there. He took Jesus up on an

exceeding high mountain and tried once more. "Again, the devil taketh him up into an exceeding high mountain, and sheweth him all the kingdoms of the world, and the glory of them; And saith unto him, All these things will I give thee, if thou wilt fall down and worship me" (vss. 8-9).

Again, Jesus quoted the Word to Satan. "...Get thee hence, Satan: for it is written, Thou shalt worship the Lord thy God, and Him only shalt thou serve"(vs 10).

Anything that exalts you and your abilities out of proportion is not good. I am concerned because some people make themselves so great, and high and mighty.

They need to turn their abilities over to Christ. Turn away, when the tempter says, "If you are a son of God cast yourself down..." Or "If you have the power of God, go back there and get those two people out of their wheel chairs...If you are a child of God — if Jesus told the truth, go back there right now, and get them up!"

I have seen many people with that type of attitude. But God does not honor a prideful attitude.

Do you realize that Jesus did not heal everybody that He passed by? He wanted to heal everybody but He did not heal them all.

Jesus healed one man when there was a whole multitude that wanted to be healed. That man had been sick for thirty-eight years. Jesus chose him only from amidst the crowd. It was not because He wanted to. He said, "I can do nothing of myself." He said, "I am dependent upon the Father, the Holy Ghost" (John 5:30 author's translation).

Know this: if the Holy Ghost told me to go back and get a person by his arms, and raise him up, it would happen. That is why we have to pray, and wait upon God, and obey the Holy Ghost.

You may say, "Well, why doesn't He tell you to do that today?"

I don't know why. All I can do is just follow God, and teach his Word until He talks to me. He will direct us individually in every situation by the Holy Ghost.

I do know that this happened once. A lady came into a church where I was ministering with knots all over her body. She could not even turn her head a certain way because of a huge knot. Her arms had been frozen by rheumatoid arthritis. I knew that woman, and I knew that she had knots all over her body — all over her arms. But I did not know she had lupus, an incurable blood disease.

The Holy Ghost said to me, "I want to heal her..." There is a difference between what I say and what the Holy Ghost says. I want you to know that when I touched that woman on the forehead, the power of God came on her, and in one moment's time she was healed instantaneously. She was a member of the First Baptist Church, but her hands and arms flew up, and every knot left her body instantly. She was healed of everything that was wrong with her, and she received the Baptism in the Holy Ghost.

This lady is still telling her wonderful story today. She went back to her doctors and they verified the fact she no longer had lupus. This miracle happened just because the Holy Ghost spoke to me. Don't let the devil get you to do some foolish thing that God or the Holy Ghost has not told you to do. Keep Jesus first in your life and follow his voice.

Do what Jesus did, and you will overcome the tempter.

Jesus overcame Satan by the Word of God, and only by the Word of God. Here are four important things that you can do to send the tempter away.

First: **Find out what the Word of God says about the situation.**

Second: **Read what God says about it in His Word, and meditate on it until you get that Word down into your spirit.**

Third: **Quote what God says about it in His Word to the devil.** Don't just quote the Scripture to yourself, quote it to the devil, because that really torments him. Just open your Bible and say, "Come over here Mr. devil. If you can read, we will read it together..." Then read the Word to him.

Fourth: **Learn to keep your mouth shut.** As you find out what God says about the situation, and you read and meditate on it until it gets down into your spirit, and you begin to say it to the devil, you are ready to do number four. Learn to keep your mouth shut, lest you add something to what the Word says. Don't get into a discussion with the devil.

You will notice that **Jesus did not get into an argument with the devil.** He didn't say, "Well, sit down here, devil, and let's talk about it." He simply quoted what the Word said. Jesus never went beyond the Word.

After you quote the Word to the devil, keep that little hole, right under your nose tightly closed. Do not say anything except the Word of God.

There have been times when I thought that I was really going to die. I might have been in some foreign place and it looked as though everything was over. I would quote what the Bible says..."With long life will he satisfy me, and show me his salvation" (Psalm 91:16). "By his stripes I am healed..." (I Peter 2:24; Isaiah 53:5).

I never go by what or how I feel. I do not get into a discussion with the devil. I find out what the Word of God says about the situation. I read God's Word, and meditate on it, and I begin to say God's Word to the devil.

In Matthew 4:11, you will find that when Jesus did all of these things the devil left him. "Then the devil leaveth him, and, behold, angels came and ministered unto him."

After you follow Jesus' example you will be doing what you are supposed to do when the tempter comes to you, and he will have to go.

Then, as the angels ministered unto Jesus, they will come and minister unto you.

In conclusion, I want to share with you a prophecy that came forth just before I began to teach on **What To Do When The Tempter Comes.**

> For I am a Healer, saith the Lord.
> Yea, and My compassion reaches out to
>   all mankind;
>   to the young and old alike.
> There are none that escape My eye:
> For I am your Creator.
> And I am your God.
> And I am your Physician.
> And nothing is too hard for me.
> Oh My children, lift up your
>   eyes unto the heavens.
> Yes, behold the heavens,
>   and the heavens of heavens.
> And did not My hand create all these,
>   saith God?
> Look about you in the world.
> Did not My hand create this?
> I am the God of all flesh.

Do not despair or lose hope.
Yea, read My Word.
Rise up in faith.
For I am a God of miracles.
And I will do that which you desire,
  saith the Lord.

BOOKS BY JOHN OSTEEN

A Miracle For Your Marriage
A Place Called There
ABC's of Faith
Believing God For Your Loved Ones
Deception! Recognizing True and False Ministries
Four Principles in Receiving From God
*Healed of Cancer by Dodie Osteen
*How To Claim the Benefits of the Will
How To Demonstrate Satan's Defeat
How To Flow in the Super Supernatural
How To Minister Healing to the Sick
*How To Receive Life Eternal
How To Release the Power of God
Keep What God Gives
Love & Marriage
Overcoming Hindrances To Receiving the Baptism in the Holy Spirit
Overcoming Opposition: How To Succeed in Doing the Will of God
    by Lisa Comes
*Pulling Down Strongholds
*Receive the Holy Spirit
Reigning in Life as a King
Rivers of Living Water
Saturday's Coming
Seven Facts About Prevailing Prayer
Seven Qualities of a Man of Faith
*Six Lies the Devil Uses To Destroy Marriages by Lisa Comes
Spiritual Food For Victorious Living
The Believer's #1 Need
The Bible Way to Spiritual Power
The Confessions of a Baptist Preacher
*The Divine Flow
*The 6th Sense...Faith
The Truth Shall Set You Free
*There Is a Miracle in Your Mouth
This Awakening Generation
Unraveling the Mystery of the Blood Covenant
*What To Do When Nothing Seems To Work
What To Do When the Tempter Comes
You Can Change Your Destiny

***Also available in Spanish.**

Please write for a complete list of prices in the John Osteen Library.
Lakewood Church • P.O. Box 23297 • Houston, Texas 77228